6.67

Never Say Ugh to a Bug

by Norma Farber
pictures by
Jose Aruego

GREENWILLOW BOOKS
A Division of
William Morrow & Company, Inc., New York

To my Concord Crowd–
who never do

Text copyright © 1961, 1963, 1976, 1977, 1978, 1979
by Norma Farber. Illustrations copyright © 1979
by Jose Aruego.
"Caterpillar Carol" was first published in *Instructor*, copyright © May 1972 by The Instructor Publications, Inc., used
by permission of the author. "Advice from a Water-Skater"
and "Oh the Toe-Test!" first appeared in *Cricket*; "Beget-
ting" (under the title "Snail"), "Left-Winged Cricket,"
"Mantis-Hood," and "Sing Wake!" (under the title "Waken
Singing") in *The Christian Science Monitor*; and "Lulla,
Wasp" (under the title "Lulla, Lulla, Lulla") in *Voices*.

Library of Congress Cataloging in Publication Data
Farber, Norma.   Never say ugh to a bug.
SUMMARY: Twenty poems about insects including
the slug, maggot, fly, grub, and others.
1. Insects –Juvenile poetry.   [1. Insects–Poetry.
2. American poetry] I. Aruego, Jose. II. Title.
PZ8.3.F224Ne   811'.5'4   78-13948   ISBN 0-688-80140-4
ISBN 0-688-84140-6 lib. bdg.

Contents

Garbage Collector's Song

Never say *Ugh!* to maggots.
　　It's not considered nice.
They're nature's things—
like coral strings,
or grains of glistening rice.

Ladybug, Be Good

Summer's over. Work is through.
Lady, get to bed.
Where your tasty meadow grew,
now a stubble rubs instead.

Dream of lice and aphides,
brood on summer scale.
Hide your wings from crystal freeze,
polka dots from bouncing hail.

Shrink from bleak and blizzard whiffs.
Barely breathe: it's best.
Ladybud, no buts and ifs.
Close your shutters, come to rest.

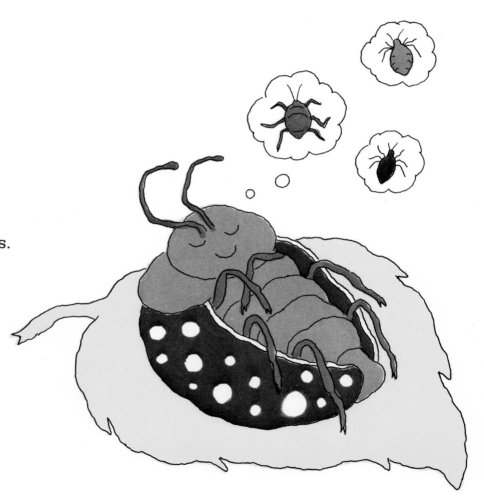

Says the Dragonfly Nymph:

My mother never gets upset,
nor tries to mend me just because
I tear my skin and leave it wet
and hanging somewhere by the claws.

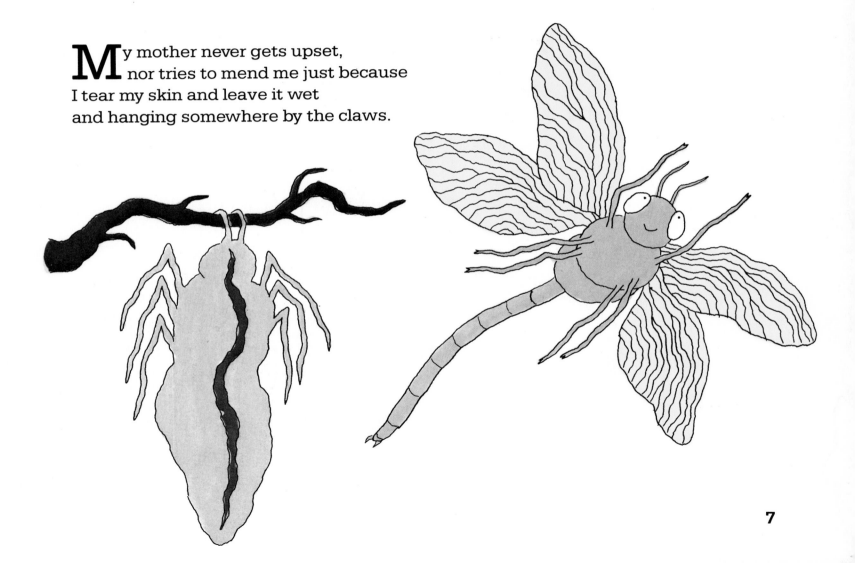

Out of the Mouths of Spittlebugs

My eggs are snug,
says the spittlebug.

On a grass, on a stem
I bundle them
in a swaddle-cloth
of downy froth.

They hatch in foam.
For them it's home.

Some eggs lie plain
on grass, on grain.
I hide my little
seeds in spittle.

8

Advice from a Water-Skater

Fasten your skates,
    my darling daughter.
Make figure eights
on top of the water.
Keep to the rule,
as I've taught you to.
Dimple the pool—
but *don't fall through!*

Begetting

Snails beget snails—
the size of nails—
with heads like tails—
in parks—in pails—
in bouquets—in bales—
on the backs of whales—
in the beaks of quails—
down riverside dales—
under snow-white sails—
in calms—in gales—
when it blows—when it hails—
when it shines—when it pales—
males—females—
in jungles—in jails—
in shavings—in shales—
near carrots—near kales—
even sent through the mails—
depositing trails—
like Turkish veils—
on runways—on rails—
on fishermen's scales.

It never fails.
Snails beget snails.

Left-Winged Cricket

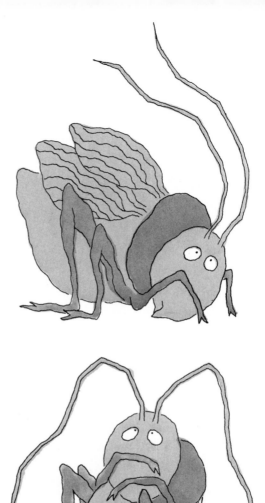

As I was going to Boston,
one sunny August day,
I heard a left-winged cricket
forlornly scrape and play.
I heard him draw a chirrup
as mournful as a moan.
A stranger music from two wings
was surely never known.

"Oh why," I asked the cricket,
"so sadly in the grass,
do you excite the pity
of people as they pass?
A cricket should be happy,
a cricket brings good cheer.
Oh can you be in point of fact
as sad as you appear?"

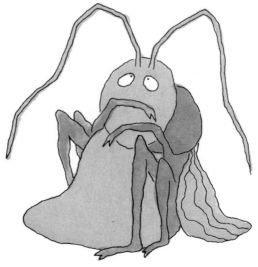

"Indeed," said he, "I suffer,
  and painfully I mind
  that I perform so otherwise
  than my own cricket-kind.
  Look how they file their ballads
  melodious and bright,
  the right upon their left wing case,
  while I—left over right!"

"No sillier thing it's possible
  to make a mountain of,
  than which wing case lies under,
  and which should lie above.
  Technique's no cart-and-horse affair,
  no do-it-right-or-die.
  That two wing cases work in time
  is what should count," said I.

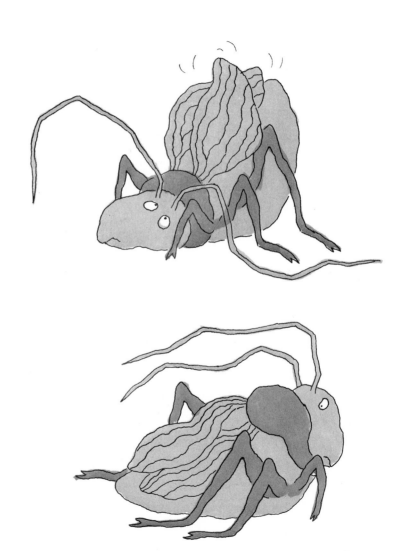

"How blind you are," the cricket cried,
"how foolish, or perverse.
  If you belittle my complaint,
  you make my matters worse.
  The sun arises in the east.
  It settles in the west.
  By right wing case on top of left
  the cricket song's expressed.

"No other way's quite cricket.
  Not if you want to claim
  the privilege of carrying
  your rightful cricket name.
  To choose is not quite cricket.
  We do as we are bid.
  Or else we'd be a grasshopper.
  Or else a katydid.

"And that's why I'm despairing.
  For since my way is wrong,
  I know I'll never execute
  a proper cricket song.
  My mother tried to change me
  and set my cases straight.
  But I was born left-over-right.
  Correction came too late."

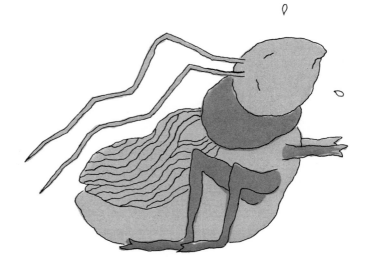

"Left-over-right, how splendid!"
cried I. "You're something new!
You've simply burst the boundaries
of that which crickets do!
By your bold innovation
all cricketdom is freed.
I'll have to write a verse or two
to celebrate your deed."

Forthwith I wrote this poem
to please the mournful mite.
I wrote it with my left hand,
since that's the way I write.
Then on I went to Boston,
for that's where I was bound.
And as I went I thought I heard
a cheerful cricket sound.

Book Louse

It's simple truth
that one sweet tooth
and another are apt to differ.

So it's hardly fair to be minding,
while *one* is enjoying the poetry, if a-
*noth*er's preferring the binding.

Caterpillar Carol

Softer than the breath of woolly bears,
   sleeping:
the sound of my velvet bellows,
creeping.
Quieter than woolly bears stretching,
bending:
the carol of my concertina,
wending....

Providing

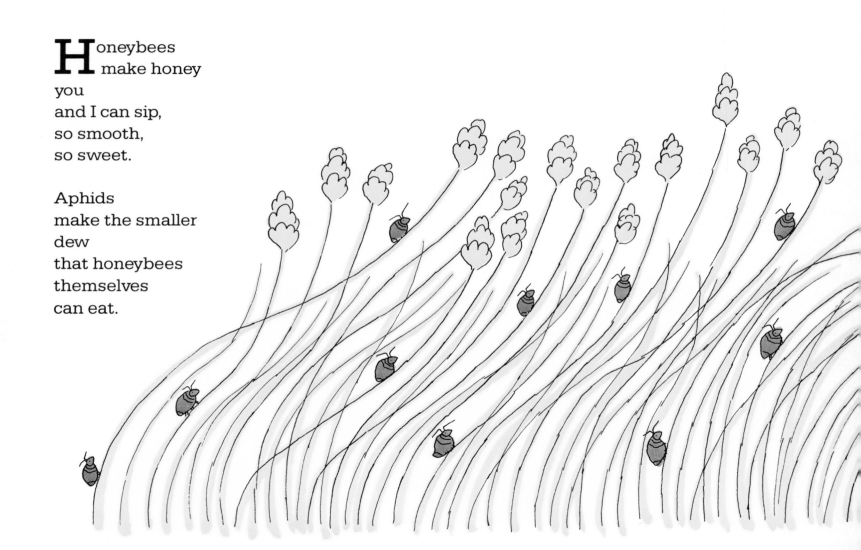

Honeybees
make honey
you
and I can sip,
so smooth,
so sweet.

Aphids
make the smaller
dew
that honeybees
themselves
can eat.

Mantis-Hood

Said the praying mantis: It says in a book,
over my shoulder I'm able to look.
Over my shoulder (it's said by a man),
look back, I'm the *only* insect that can.

Said the praying mantis: My children, be good.
Grow up to do all that you properly should.
Grow into your mantis-hood wiser and older,
so *you* will be fit to look over your shoulder.

21

Mystery of the Spider's Web

Nightfalling rain.
Your umbrella's plain
to be seen, stretched wide.

Sun before noon.
Too soon, too soon
the cloth has dried.

Where is it?
Did you close it
in a closet,
or lose it?

Sing Wake!

Listen and hear!
   A winter-sleeper,
loudest and littlest,
the one-inch peeper—
while others yawn
with voices vacant—
wakens singing,
and sings awakened!

Slow Slalom

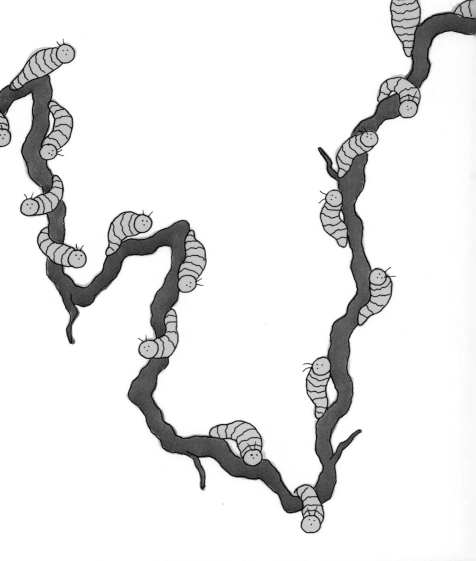

Slithering in a
slippery
   slowful
      sleek
   slalom
      slurring

            slantwise under a
      slab
   slicing down
slits of
   slidden soil
      slinking
         slickery

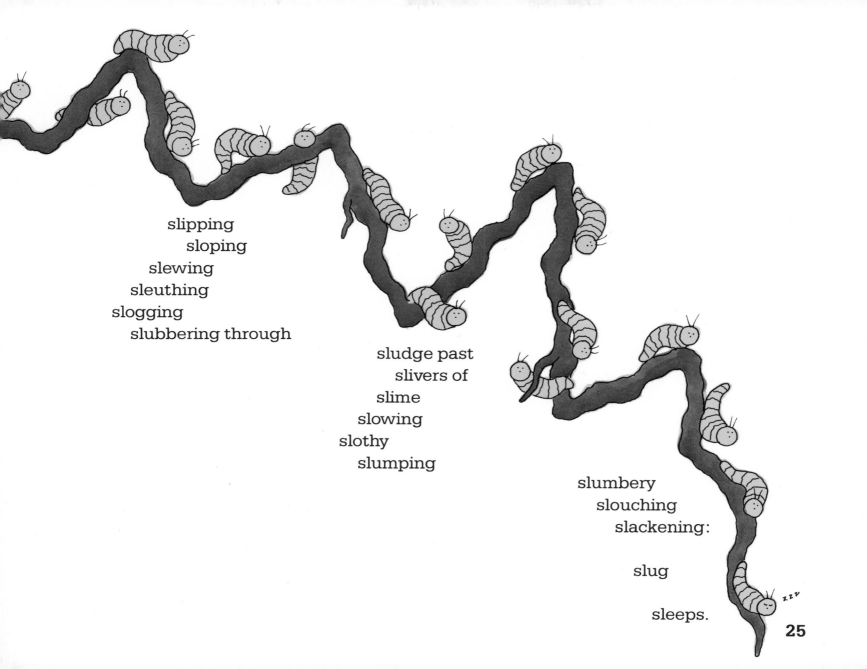

slipping
sloping
slewing
sleuthing
slogging
slubbering through

sludge past
slivers of
slime
slowing
slothy
slumping

slumbery
slouching
slackening:

slug

sleeps.

25

Lulla, Wasp

His secret's bound
in swaddle-skin.
No sight, no sound
of waspikin.

Dig soft his room,
his window close.
In such small gloom
tomorrow grows.

Cocoon will keep
till thread must break.
Sleep, larva, sleep,
and winged awake.

End of Season

Twang,
the mosquito sang.
Not a very strong
song.

Ping,
went his sting.
Just a weak
tweak.

Ho, hum, time to shinny
up a pitcher plant. In he

creeps.

Sleeps.

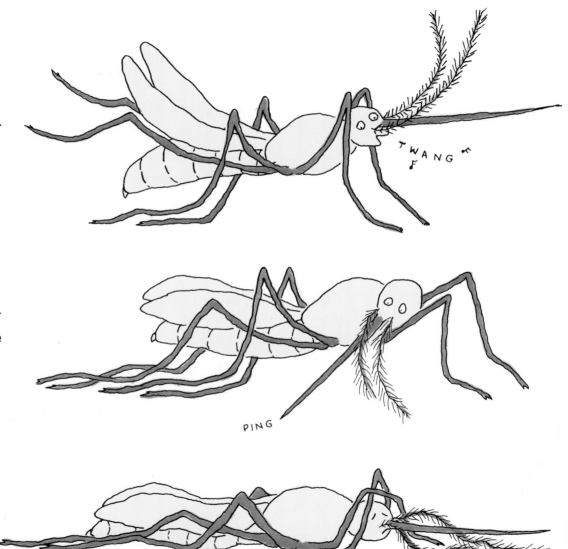

Make Way!

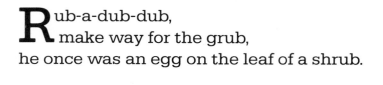

Rub-a-dub-dub,
make way for the grub,
he once was an egg on the leaf of a shrub.

Now he can crawl,
don't let him fall.
Soon he will fly in a tarlatan shawl.

Snorkeling

Down in the pond
there's a scorpion slim,
who lies at the bottom
and looks at the brim.

Down in the pond
by the weeds and the slime,
he puts up his snorkel
and passes the time.

29

A Very Sharp Tongue in His Cheek

The Burgundy Snail
   which is two inches long
has thirty-five thousands of teeth
on his tongue.

With so much equipment,
he chews—without question—
sufficiently fine
for a careful digestion.

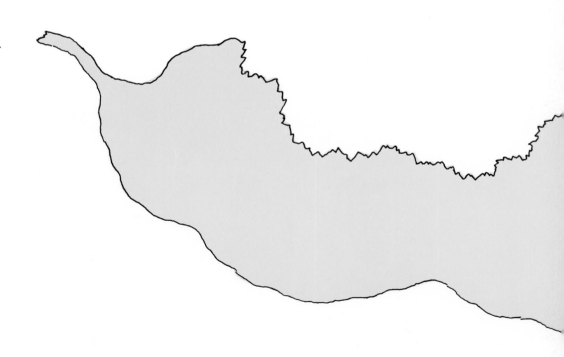

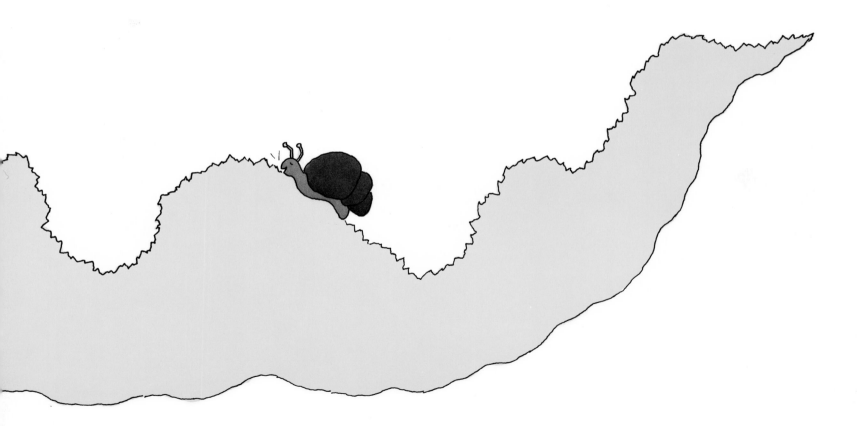

31

Oh the Toe-Test!

The fly, the fly,
   in the wink of an eye,
can taste with his feet
if the syrup is sweet
or the bacon is salty.
Oh is it his fault he
gets toast on his toes
as he tastes as he goes?